THE ENGLISH OAK
QUERCUS ROBUR

The Oak, through its character, history, culture and uses, stands as the quintessential English tree, and unquestionably one of the greatest organisms of the English landscape. There can be few hearts or souls that are not drawn in some way to the spirit of this dendrological English King. A magisterial tree, at the same time attracting the respect owed to the protective influence associated with a benign father. In its turn it symbolises much of the English character which, like the tree has sustained itself through the centuries of history. Strength and endurance being the key qualities that have characterised both the Oak and the Englishman, and through this mutuality, the tree's serendipitous bequest has been employed in any number of ingenious ways, both spiritually and materially. The nation and the tree have grown alongside in a mutually beneficial collaboration. From artefacts to flagships, humble floorboards to soaring timber roofs, the common door, thrones, the hammer beam, farmsteads, churches, palaces and amongst the emblems, a brave man's badge.

'Three centuries he grows, and three he stays

supreme in state, and in three more he decays.'

Dryden (1631-1700)

To many ancient tribes the Oak was believed not only to be the first tree God created, but it wa the Oak from which sprang the human race. Not surprising then that such renowned mytholog led over time to the tree becoming one of the most widely venerated of sacred plants. Acros many cultures it has symbolised the inner fire of courage; nobility of spirit; faith; independence longevity; royalty; stability, honour and reward. Its reputation for being a sacred tree of grea strength has come to equate it with durability, antiquity, long life and fortitude, giving strength and courage to carry on and through a particular kind of self-determination, to fight and endure the greatest difficulties.

The Victorian botanist Loudon's description epitomises the oak as the 'emblem of grandeur, strength and duration; of force that resists, as the lion is of force that acts.' In the language of flowers oak leaves were known as The crown of morality and virtue. It was an ancient tradition for those who had saved the lives of others to be given wreathes made of oak leaves. How appropriate that this decorative recognition and award came down the centuries to the First World War, when servicemen and women who were Mentioned in Despatches were given an Oak Leaf emblem, symbolising the courage associated with the award. This decoration was carried forward to the Royal Marines in the Second World War.

'*Great oaks from little acorns grow*' is an apt and popular saying and reminds us that '*every majestic oak was once a nut who stood his ground*', symbolising the huge potential there is in small things. E.F. Schumacker, the 20th century pioneer for green economics, beautifully describes this metaphorically powerful message of the Oak: 'Our ordinary mind always tries to persuade us that we are nothing but acorns and that our greatest happiness will be to become bigger, fatter, shinier acorns; but that is of interest only to pigs. Our faith gives us knowledge of something better: that we can become *oak* trees.'

The Oak is one of the most important trees of European mythology, covering the Greeks, Romans, Celts, Druids, Anglo-Saxons, Germanic and Norse tribes. It stood as an all encompassing power, and in some of these cultures it was a common belief that their gods lived in the trees, the roots delving as deep into the underworld as its branches reached for the heavens.

To our far off ancestors the tree was sacred to many of their sky gods, such as Jove and even became known as Jove's tree although was quite wrongly deemed to be safe from lightning strikes. In Classical times it was called *The Tree of Life*. To the Druids it was the *Celestial Tree*, while to the Chinese it represented masculine strength, and in Finland, as late as the 19th century it was called simply *God's Tree*!

The Greeks had a long tradition of venerating the Oak. At Eleusis it was oak leaves that were used for the symbolic crowns during the Sacred Mysteries, while Dodona in Epirus, was a sanctuary of Zeus to which people travelled in order to consult the sacred oak tree that grew there. Over time Dodona became famous as a place to receive oracles, the rustling of the oak leaves were believed to be the god's voice speaking to the suppliants and according to the Greek poet Hesiod, priestesses took the form of doves and lived in the hollow oak trunks from where they gave prophesies to pilgrims. This led to all oaks being known as sacred to Zeus, who being the father of the Greek gods then became known also as the father of all trees, and through history the Oak has continued to represent fatherly influence, with its ruling planet appropriately being Jupiter.

In Rome there were many oak groves in and around the city, and over time they became established as sanctuaries or holy places. In the 1st century, Pliny wrote about witnessing Druid altars set up under oak trees for the performance of rites, again the belief being that the trees inspired prophecy.

Further east in Palestine, the Hebrews also revered the oak as sacred as it was under an oak near Hebron that Abraham met and communed with Jehovah's three angels. This illustrious tree became known as *The Oak of Mamre*. In 1868, some two thousand years later, the Russian Church acquired the historic site, founding the Monastery of the Holy Trinity nearby, and prior to the Russian Revolution it was an important place of pilgrimage, being the only active Christian shrine in the area of Hebron. There is a legend that predicted that the Oak would die before the appearance of the so called Anti-Christ: the tree has been dead since 1996!

The Greek word for oak was *Druz*, from which the name Druid was derived and so the Druids became known as the *wise men of oak*. They revered the tree and through it they believed that they could interpret the will of the gods. However it was the Celtic name for oak - *Duir*, derived from the Sanskrit *Dwr* - meaning door and its derivative *Dur* (the actual word for oak), that spans Indo-European languages and is roughly translated as both *strong* (as in durable) and *door*. Perhaps a synthesis of these derivatives befitting the tree could be *strong door of wisdom!*

In the Celtic year the Oak stands midway at Summer Solstice, symbolising the doorway to the second half of the year and the fulfilment of hidden potential. The Celts revered the oak, and at the winter solstice chose it for the burning of the Yule log in the ceremony to attract the sun's return to warm the earth. Celtic marriages were believed to be blessed if they took place under an oak, but when the Christian church forbade such heathen activities, couples completed the church ceremony then gathered under the oak where they danced, cut crosses in the tree's bark and consumed a drink made from the acorns. At Brampton in Cumbria such practice persisted into the 19th century, and Oaks are still employed at marriage blessings today.

The Oak gave special virtue to other plants that grew on it, such as the Polypoda fern and mistletoe and if gold berried mistletoe appeared in the branches of a tree some believed that it had appeared as a result of lightning flashes from the gods of the sky and was a manifestation of their love for the oak. It was also believed that the tree acted as a lightning charm and was doubly effective if it had mistletoe growing in it. If a tree *was* struck by lightning the blackened splinters were sought as charms against further lightning strikes. Simple twigs, acorns or oak apples were placed in dwellings right up until the 20th century, in the belief that they offered protection. The familiar acorn shaped toggles on window blinds belong to that tradition.

The reality is that the Oak is actually more prone to lightning strikes than other trees, and this may be because of its low electrical resistance. However, they do usually survive and indeed can even thrive after being struck, becoming known as *lightning oaks*.

In Shamanic teaching, a bolt of lightning is believed to impart great spiritual illumination, and this connects well with the tree being both a door into wisdom and to the mysteries associated with the sun and its festivals, and its predisposition to lightning strikes.

Tolstoy vividly describes an oak being struck by lightning in his novel *Anna Karenina*: 'Suddenly there was a glare of light, the whole earth seemed on fire and the vault of heaven cracked overhead. Opening his blinded eyes, to his horror the first thing Levin saw.... was the uncannily altered position of the green crest of the familiar oak in the middle of the copse. "Can it have been struck?" The thought had barely time to cross his mind when, gathering speed, the oak disappeared behind the other trees, and he heard the crash of the great tree falling on the others.'

An early English description gives more detail: '...when a oake is falling, before it falls it gives a kind of shriekes or groanes that may be heard a mile off, as it were the genus of the oake lamenting...'

The forces of nature assaulting the oak was one thing but there were strong superstitions associated with man interfering with the tree;, and there are many stories of illness, accident and death befalling those who abused or felled oaks. These trees were not to be tampered with.

The 19th century essayist Thomas Carlyle describes how 'when the oak is felled the whole forest echoes with its fall, but a hundred acorns are sown in silence by an unnoticed breeze.'

Daniel Defoe was able to find few words to describe the Great Storm of 1703 which raged across Britain for a week with 120mph winds: 'No pen could describe it, nor tongue express it, nor thought conceive it unless by one in the extremity of it'. The hurricane saw the demise of even the mightiest oaks which lay blasted like fallen warriors on the forest floor. Four thousand oaks were felled in the New Forest alone, three thousand in the Forest of Dean. But the cause of the great vegetable patriarch, that had for so long represented the bulwark of the country's liberty, was championed at the end of that century when viewed as a man's patriotic duty to plant trees, *oak mania* gripped the country. Across the land there was rampant acorn fever, especially among the gentry, one of whom Thomas Johnes, Lord Lieutenant of Cardiganshire, planted a staggering 922.000 oaks over six years at the turn of the century.

It has long been taken for granted that the oak is England's national tree and right through history it has flourished as a powerful and emotive English emblem. It is less than five hundred years ago, during the reign of Henry VIII that a good third of England was still covered by this king of trees, so it is not surprising that it was not only the stuff of legends but the source of a whole history of imagery.

Two majestic specimens, now gnarled with age, *Gog* and *Magog* near Glastonbury, were named after the last two surviving giants known in pre-Christian Britain as father-god and mother-goddess. The famous *Major* Oak in Sherwood Forest is dated between 800 and 1000 years, and in its hollowed out trunk Robin Hood was reputed to have had his hideout. Its limbs may now need the support of a number of beams, with its glory days long gone, but it is listed by the National Tree Council as one of the nation's fifty top trees.

The Oak's reputation for being practically indestructible is born out by excavated logs from thousand year old peat bogs that are still fit for rough building work, while on the River Severn there are breakwaters still fit for purpose which are said to be the result of the Romans depositing piles of oak on these sites.

In 1982 history was brought spectacularly to the surface when the iconic *Mary Rose* was raised from the depths of the sea. She was built in 1511 of oak, taking some six hundred trees for her construction and was said to be Henry VIII's favourite galleon. After only just over 30 years of service she was sunk in 1545 in the Solent while leading the attack on a French invasionary force.

As recently as 1999 the remarkable discovery of the 4050 year old *Seahenge* was made on the Norfolk coast by a man walking his dog! It consisted of a circular formation of 55, two meter high oak posts with a central boss, of seven meters high, all preserved in an anaerobic state. These historical examples are testament to the unvanquishable nature of the wood, and also to its extraordinary tolerance to water.

The qualities, both physical and spiritual, for which the oak has for so long been recognised have found their expression in the daily life of men over thousands of years. In many different traditions it was common practice for meetings and religious ceremonies to be convened under an oak tree; the symbolic figurehead of wisdom, strength and authority. As an extension of this reputation, historically it was oak that was chosen to provide stout, resilient and beautiful doors, spiritually endowing those who passed the threshold with strength and security. Stretching back to early Bronze Age man, coffins were made from hollowed out oak, the strength of the wood, materially and symbolically ensuring the dead a safe passage journeying from this world to the next.

For centuries oak was the most important forest tree and although in Europe it was also a prolific and important species it has nevertheless remained a peculiarly, and most particular *English* tree, a vital resource examples of which were woven into the fabric of the nation. There is the Anglo-Saxon twenty-seven metre oak ship excavated at Sutton Hoo. King Arthur's famous Round Table - eighteen feet across and made from what must have been the bole of a very large oak - still to be seen in the Great Hall in Winchester. Elizabeth I's fleet that defeated the Armada. Shakespeare's Globe Theatre. The great roof of Westminster Hall, for which some 650 tons of oak was brought up the Thames to provide timber for the heavy hammer beam roof, carved posts, rafters, trusses, braces and adorning angels. There were the aptly named *wooden walls of England* - the ships of the Navy headed by Nelson's *Victory* that defeated the joint French and Spanish Navy at Trafalgar in 1805. Sadly it was only nineteen years after this great naval victory that these magnificent vessels were obsolete, but the words of David Garrick's famous shanty, adopted by the Navy as their official anthem, rang out long after their demise!
'Heart of Oak are our ships,
Heart of Oak are our men'.

Oak has not only provided an outstanding natural material source, but has found its way into national iconography with, for example the English sixpences and shillings engraved with the distinctive oak spray. In 1895 the National Trust was founded, and in 1896 they purchased their first historic building, the near derelict Alfriston Clergy House in Sussex, for which they paid a mere £10! Inspired by a carved wooden cornice in the hall of the building, they took its subject of the acorn and oak spray as the inspiration for their iconic logo to champion the endurance of places that represent the heart of Britain. As recently as 2006 the Conservative Party replaced its torch of freedom logo with a stylised oak tree aspiring to represent a country of modern but abiding values. The Oak's qualities of strength, renewal, growth and endurance, along with its essential *Englishness* fitted the bill!

During the Middle Ages the ubiquitous oak was the mainstay material in the construction of a whole range of building. Even the minutiae of the tree - leaves, acorns, galls - finding their place in most English Cathedrals and many Parish Churches. The wood was also commonly used for interior panelling, most famously in the Debating Chamber of the House of Commons. Decoratively oak (often gilded) was to be found on door knockers, shutters, bridles and generally on churches and houses alike. However, all this intensive use over the centuries, with the felling of the great forests, that in Neolithic times had provided the bulk of tree cover across vast areas of Britain, was to take a heavy toll on the Oak population across the country.

A piece of English history was shaped by an oak tree when in 1651 Charles II, escaping from his defeat at the battle of Worcester hid from the Roundheads in a tree that came to be known as the *Boscobel Oak*. Charles' later escape from Brighton Beach may well be the origin through the 19th century of the local fishing boats being decorated with oak branches annually on that same day. As a result of having been delivered safely from the arms of the oak, the day on which the king was restored to his throne - 29th. May 1660 - became known variously as *Royal Oak Day, Oak Apple Day* and *Restoration Day,* and when Charles re-entered London, troops and citizens marked the event by wearing oak in their hat bands. From this time pubs popularly adopted the now common name of *Royal Oak*. The original tree that saved the monarch was plundered during his exile, but a scion of it was preserved at Boscobel. This tree certainly saved the King's life, but only twenty five years after his restoration Somerset men from the Duke of Monmouth's army were hanged on the Heddon Oak, near Crowcombe. Their murders during the bloody Monmouth Rebellion gave rise to stories that told of rhythmic sounds of bodies swinging from the branches in the wind, the clanking of chains and the moaning of men choking to death. The tree unsurprisingly was known as one of the *gallows trees*.

History has played its part in the planting of oak trees, and it is a long standing tradition even today to plant oak to mark a life or an event of importance. It was Lord Burghley - Queen Elizabeth 1's Treasurer - who first seriously planted oaks, reputedly selecting the biggest acorns in the belief that these would grow the biggest trees. There is a touching story that in 1798 the then eleven year old poet Lord Byron chose to plant an oak when he first visited his ancestral home of Newstead, noting that 'as it flourished, so should he'.

The most common planting of oaks were for hundreds of years those planted to mark out parish boundaries, providing an irrevocable presence right across the country. Clergy and parishioners also practised the beating of the parish bounds which was a way of establishing boundaries before mapping was developed. In many English counties some of these 'guardian' oaks are still known by the nickname of *Gospel Oak* harking back to times when, during Rogationtide (the ancient festival that invoked a blessing on fields and stock) Psalms and Gospel truths were chanted under the boughs of such trees. Herrick's poem bears witness to this tradition.

'Dearest, bury me

Under that holy oke, or Gospel Tree;

Where, though thou see'st not, thou may'st think upon

Me, when you yearly go'st Procession'

Herrick 1591 - 1674

England, more than any other European country, has a proud and moving legacy of ancient oaks. There can be few parishes (on reasonably low lying land) that do not house at least one 250 year old oak, many of which have some history and or custom associated with them. But there are also innumerable far older specimens located around the country. Near Hereford, for instance, there is the Eardisley Oak, alive though hollow with a girth of thirty-four feet and believed to be well over 1000 years old. Another 1000 year old is the Bowthorpe Oak in Lincolnshire, and the Marton Oak in Cheshire is possibly even older. One of the largest oaks in Britain (and probably in Europe) is the Fredville Oak in Kent. It was aptly known as Majesty and dates back to at the latest the Elizabethan period. Most of the oldest specimens of oak and the ones with the biggest trunks are trees that for hundred's of years were pollarded to provide a source of good timber, and in many cases this has contributed to their longevity.

A renowned old tree is the Meavy Oak in the Dartmoor village it is named after. It was planted during King John's reign (late 12th century) and in its mature years, during the 1800's, a platform was erected over the clipped top of the magnificent tree, on which tables and chairs were set for dancing and feasting. It still stands, but withered somewhat, its partying days over!

Another famous character tree is the Conquerors Oak (William the Conqueror), a hollowed out giant, twenty-seven feet in circumference, in which it was reported a lunch party took place accommodating '...at least twenty persons with standing room, and ten or twelve might sit comfortably down to dinner...' This tree is in Windsor Great Park amongst some one hundred ancient pollarded oaks, that date back to the Middle Ages known affectionately as the dodders.

The 19th century diarist Francis Kilvert described another group of ancients, the thousand year old pollarded oaks of Moccas Park in Herefordshire '...grey, gnarled low-browed, knock-kneed, bowed, bent, huge, strange, long-armed, deformed, hunch-backed, misshapen oak men!

The Oak is host to an extensive range of wildlife including many tree fungi and lichen, oak woodland being particularly favoured by *Stinkhorn* fungi. The tree also has a particular feature of producing *Lammas shoots* at high summer which extends its capability of holding on to much of its foliage through the last months of the year. This makes it especially attractive to animals who have chosen it for shelter, as well as offering a rich storehouse of nourishment supporting some three hundred insect species.

Given its dense crown and particularly deep root system it is hardly surprising that the tree has a considerable water requirement. An average tree draws some twenty gallons of water a day through its network of lateral roots. In Mundon, Essex however, stands the petrified forest of ancient oaks that were killed by imbibing the salt waters of encroaching tides. First mentioned in the Domesday Book, they later escaped being felled for the building of the naval fleet against the Spanish Armada, disqualified by their twisted trunks. A slower death overtook them, although many are still standing, dead but defiant, a strangely haunting legacy.

While the oak tree is indisputably iconic, the acorn represents itself independent of its parent as potently symbolic, embodying a delightful and exquisite piece of natural engineering long imitated by jewellers, woodworkers and sculptors. In Irish folklore the acorn may have been associated with being the Leprechaun's pipe, but in the real world the acorn is the life-giving fruit of the oak and aptly symbolised both fecundity and immortality to the Nordic tribes to whom it was an important part of their staple diet. Likewise the Druids ate acorns as part of their preparation for delivering prophesies. As cereal grains became established the nutritious acorn was relegated to the feeding of pigs, and for centuries there was the widespread practice of *pannage* - grazing pigs in oak woodland. Acorn crops are variable but when the trees are heavily laden with acorns it is taken as a sign that a hard winter will follow. In such years it has been calculated that a single Jay can on average collect and store for the winter an amazing 4600 acorns. Small wonder that in the avian world acorns have been such a favourite with Jays.

The use of oak in herbal medicine is reflected well in the Doctrine of Signatures with its important focus on the feet! Oak bark and leaves were long employed as a salve for ailing feet and on a deeper level were a stimulating aid for directing one's way in life.

The powdered bark proved beneficial in the treatment of early onset TB, and there was an old country cure for toothache that required a man to drive a nail into the tree, symbolically leaving his pain with the tree. Another country maxim which is more relevantly reliable refers to the coming into leaf of the oak:

Ash before Oak we'll surely get a soak. Oak before Ash it'll be just a splash

Over time in construction work oak was replaced by the inferior elm and later by cast iron, steel and concrete. Nevertheless, the oak's reputation endures undisputed and is now undergoing a strong revival among both builders and craftsmen. It is ironic though that most oak wood being used in Britain has to be imported from Europe as English oak is sadly in such short supply. That being the case, and given the strong ties the British have always had with the stalwart oak, it has fiercely and often successfully been protected by bodies of protestors, desperately fighting to save venerable and not so venerable oaks from bulldozers, and from those who would replace their great beauty and enduring grandeur with concrete and tarmac.

Such protest highlights an environmental and historical imperative to ensure that the nation's great icon is awarded the honour and protection it deserves.